The Highwayman's Revenge

Written by Cath Howe

Illustrated by Keino

Published by Pearson Education Limited, Edinburgh Gate, Harlow, Essex, CM20 2JE
Registered company number: 872828

www.pearsonschools.co.uk

Text © Cath Howe 2012

Designed by Bigtop
Original illustrations © Pearson Education Limited 2012
Illustrated by Keino

The right of Cath Howe to be identified as author of this work has been asserted by her in accordance with the Copyright, Designs and Patents Act 1988.

First published 2012

20
10 9

British Library Cataloguing in Publication Data
A catalogue record for this book is available from the British Library

ISBN 978 0 435 07575 0

Printed and bound in China by Golden Cup

Acknowledgements
We would like to thank the children and teachers of Bangor Central Integrated Primary School, NI; Bishop Henderson C of E Primary School, Somerset; Brookside Community Primary School, Somerset; Cheddington Combined School, Buckinghamshire; Cofton Primary School, Birmingham; Dair House Independent School, Buckinghamshire; Deal Parochial School, Kent; Holy Trinity Catholic Primary School, Chipping Norton; Lawthorn Primary School, North Ayrshire; Newbold Riverside Primary School, Rugby and Windmill Primary School, Oxford for their invaluable help in the development and trialling of the Bug Club resources.

Every effort has been made to contact copyright holders of material reproduced in this book. Any omissions will be rectified in subsequent printings if notice is given to the publisher.

Contents

Chapter 1

I lay in bed, my eyes wide open. I kept thinking about burning the strange glove in Dad's bonfire; how it had twisted and hissed. I remembered how my cousin Zac had changed when he'd worn the glove:

bullying people, breaking things, being violent and mean. I had been right to burn it. Now no one could ever wear it again.

But something felt wrong.

At dawn, I couldn't stand it any longer. Down in the garden, on the dewy grass, I found a stick and poked the powdery remains of the bonfire. I felt a lump in the centre of the ashes and lifted it out in a shower of charred dust. It was the long, black leather glove.

I rubbed it on my dressing gown, half expecting it to fall apart, but instead it felt firm and heavy. As the fingers spread out, a sweet spicy smell began to waft upwards. I gasped. The smell was just as strong as before, and the glove was now gleaming. Dread mounted in my chest. Impossible! I'd seen the glove curl and twist among the hungry flames the day before. How could it possibly have survived the fire?

The faint whispering began again, *"Wear me, wear me!"*

I shuddered and held the glove at arm's length, trying to stay away from that fantastic spicy smell.

I'd failed; I hadn't destroyed the glove, even after a whole night in the smouldering embers of the fire.

I dropped the glove, ran back to my room and grabbed the coffin-box which had been the glove's home when we'd found it in the old pub. When I got back to the garden, I threw the glove into the box, slammed on the lid and wrapped the box in some empty compost bags in the shed.

That was better. I couldn't smell the smell. Above all, I had to stop my cousin Zac finding out; he believed the glove had been destroyed.

Over the next few days, I worried. I kept checking that the glove was still in the shed, but whenever I unwrapped it, the smell seemed to draw me in closer and closer. I tried not to touch it. Each time, I forced myself just to wrap it up again.

Zac seemed cold and distant. He wouldn't speak to me, and I was walking to school alone since I had taken his beloved glove away. But our school half-term was about to begin, so I was looking forward to the holiday. Our families always went away together at half-term, so surely Zac and I would be friends again then. But the day before we were due to leave, Mum came into the living room, stony-faced.

"That was Aunt Jean on the phone. They're not coming with us on holiday."

"Not coming?" my brother Dillon gasped. "Is Zac coming on his own?"

Dillon loves being with Zac.

"None of them are coming," Mum said, frowning. "Jean says Zac's doing a tennis course instead."

My heart sank.

"But why?" Dillon whined.

Mum looked over at me. "I can't think.

Have you two had a quarrel?"
How could I explain?
I shrugged. "Dunno," I murmured.

Our half-term holiday was a washout
with Dillon whingeing on about Zac.

"This is that bit of beach where we
normally do the stone-skimming. Don't
bother, Shona, it's only fun when it's the
three of us …"

"If Zac was here, we could all go on the
model railway …"

"It's your fault Zac didn't come with us,
Shona," he said one evening. "I wish Zac
had come and we'd left *you* behind."

"Oh, just go away!" I shouted. I felt bad
enough already, without Dillon reminding
me about Zac all the time.

I ended up mooching about collecting
shells and rocks. And thinking. If the
glove could still make me want to wear it,
maybe it was still calling to Zac, too.

It was as if we'd both caught an infection, only he had it worse. That had to be why Zac wasn't speaking to me any more, surely? Well, he wasn't getting that horrible glove back; not even if he screamed his lungs off!

Somewhere in the back of my mind I kept wondering why that glove was so powerful. Did it really belong to a highwayman? What had happened to him?

The day before the end of the very long, not fun half-term holiday, we were eating our tea in a café. The weather had been hot and dry and Mum was worrying about the new seedlings she'd planted before we came away.

"Zac said he'd pop in and do some watering," she said. "I hope he remembers."

I nearly choked on my chicken pie. Zac in our garden! Zac in our shed!

"Don't worry, he will." Dad said. "He seemed really keen."

Oh no! Of course he was willing. He must have sensed that the glove was still around somewhere!

I couldn't wait to be home. As soon as we got there, I rushed out to the shed.

I found the box.

Empty.

Chapter 2

I had no one to walk to school with; no friendly cousin, just a terrible feeling about what Zac would be doing now he'd got the glove back. And it certainly wasn't playing tennis.

I was dreading the first day back at school. Zac and I are in different classes so I didn't see him that day in lessons. But we had a rehearsal after school for the highwayman play. Zac strode into the hall, caught my eye but looked away. His left arm was thickly bandaged.

"What's happened to your arm, Zac?" Mr Costello asked.

"Sports injury," Zac said. He grabbed the rest of his costume.

"How did you hurt it, Zac?" I asked him.

"Bother me not, you nest of worms!" Zac said roughly, his eyes gleaming.

The bandage coiled away onto the floor. Underneath, Zac had the black leather glove on. He scooped the bandage into his pocket and strode up the steps onto the stage. He'd been wearing the glove all day in school!

Ella rolled her eyes and giggled. "Nest of worms!" she said to me. "Why can't Zac talk properly?"

"Don't ask me," I said, but the dread was already growing in my chest. Zac seemed a complete stranger.

Mr Costello seemed really pleased to see everyone back.

"Right, now, we've had a week's holiday and there are only two weeks of rehearsal left, so I want everyone on board and firing on all cylinders. No monkey business." He glanced at Zac.

I was still haunted by Robert's agonised face when Zac had attacked him a couple of weeks ago. Should I have told everyone that Robert had been too terrified to carry on playing the highwayman?

Mr Costello continued, "Zac has assured me that he's desperate to be

our highwayman and, since he showed
such exceptional talent, I'm giving him
another chance after what he assures me
was a moment of madness ... So, no funny
business, Zac. You're on a warning. Now,
let's make a start."

Zac didn't even speak to me as I was
tethering my model horse to a cardboard
bush. A team of people had been making
Sir Stanley's coach in the art room for
weeks out of the frame of an old sofa.
It even had doors that opened. Miss
Sheridan from the Art Department had
painted it and added a fancy curtain.

"Right, everyone on stage," called Mr Costello. "Our vicious highwayman holds up the stagecoach on the common. Molly and Richard, you are obviously Lady Penelope and Lord Stanley travelling inside and are about to be robbed. And Shona, you help the highwayman by stashing away all the stolen things in the forest hideout. So, everyone in character? Super!" He clapped his hands, then paused. "I'm not sure there's much point in a highwayman with only one glove, though."

"Fret ye not!" Zac shouted. "I'll keep looking for another." He rammed the three-cornered hat lower on his head.

Mr Costello smiled. "Now, that's cool. I can see you're getting into role with your words there, Zac. You're living in the forest, so let me see you prowling."

The stage was drowned in silvery moonlight. We pushed the coach into the centre and I hid behind it.

"From his misty lair, deep in the trees,
He hears the coach wheels rattling,"
said Ella.

Zac stood behind the cardboard bush, twitching. I kept getting whiffs of that delicious smell coming from his glove.

"From the shadows the villain springs,
The wildest beast is he.
Now leaping on the carriage top
To smite the grooms with glee,"
Ella continued.

Zac leaped up onto the top of the
coach. He looked amazing. He waved his
plastic dagger, like a wrestler at the side
of the ring waiting to attack his opponent.
Then he reached down and grabbed a
sack of valuables, with a "Ah, ha!" of
triumph.

"Love it, love it!"
Mr Costello called.

Chink, **Chink**.

Zac threw the
sack down
to me.

"*Here's a pretty penny or two!*" I said.

I was supposed to pretend the sack was heavy. But today, the sack almost pulled my arms off; it really *was* heavy. And chinking? But it couldn't be; it only had rolled-up newspapers in!

My heart jumped. I tugged loose the rope fastening and thrust my hand inside. Wads and wads of newspapers. I grabbed the neck of the sack and lifted it up again. Now it was light as air. How on earth …?

I looked up at Zac.

"How did you do that?" I called. "Zac … please …!"

But Zac was wrestling with two stuffed dummies made to look like the grooms.

He held one above his head and stabbed it with his dagger, then threw it down onto the stage.

Thuddddd.

Zac was making deep slashes in the red waistcoat. Hang on; how could he? That dagger was a plastic one from the props box and its blade was blunt. But in the pale stage lighting, the blade seemed to be glinting like metal. Panic rose in my chest as I watched Zac casually toss the dagger down onto the stage.

Molly leaned out of the coach and peered at the dagger. "It looks really sharp!" she yelped.

"What's going on?" Mr Costello called.

"Molly says the dagger's sharp," I called. "Zac, what did you do to the dagger? Get down!"

Zac winked. *See the power I have?* he said.

I rushed over and picked up the dagger. In my hand it was just blunt, grey plastic. Molly began to wail. "That was horrid. That dagger was really sharp. I know it was."

She clambered out of the coach. "What? Right. Everybody stop!" Mr Costello shouted. "What do you mean, the dagger was really sharp? Zac, Molly, I want you both here this minute!"

"*No!*" cried Zac, still high up on the coach roof.

"*These are my spoils now!*"

"What did you say?" Mr Costello bellowed.

I grabbed at Zac's legs but he sprang away from me. He shook his fist.

"Don't shake your fist at me, Zac!" Fury rose inside me. "How dare you!"

Zac jumped off the top of the coach and ran to the middle of the stage, still shaking his gloved fist.

"Beware!" he shouted, spinning on his heels, clenching his fist and glaring at everyone on stage. *"When you hanged me, you fools, you forgot one thing; the grim remains of my evil life, my gauntlet. It lives on, indestructible, cursed through all eternity. It will always be waiting to re-ignite the past. Beware! Ha ha ha ha."*

The evil laugh echoed around the hall. There was a stunned silence. Then Mr Costello shouted, "Lovely improvisation, Zac, but you've been told to stop!"

Richard climbed out of the coach. Zac strode towards him, with a terrible snarl on his face. I suddenly realised what came next in our play; the highwayman attacks Lord Stanley!

Panic welled up inside me. I remembered Zac's vicious attack on Robert and knew that Richard was in *real* danger.

A few seconds was all Zac needed …

"Help! Stop him!" I screamed, rushing towards my cloaked cousin in the centre of the stage. "He's going to hurt someone!"

Chapter 3

Everyone gasped.

I ran straight at Zac's outstretched glove and whacked it.

Zac spun round, his eyes full of burning rage. He flung out his arms as if to strike me, but I dodged away.

Shouts rang out all around me.

"What's happening?"

"Get away!"

"Run!"

"Get down!"

"Get out!"

As Zac lunged towards some of the other actors, Ella started screaming. Mr Costello backed out into the wings, shouting, "Everyone clear the stage! Right now!"

I rushed at Zac. Miss Sheridan was blocking his way, reaching out and grabbing him, but he jumped out of her grasp and leaped inside the coach. I jumped in after him. I had to get that glove. The coach began to rock wildly as we fought.

My arm got twisted in Zac's cape and for a moment I was up against his terrible spitting face.

"You'll never get this glove away from me!" he hissed.

We were flung suddenly towards the door with a huge crunching sound as the coach collapsed. It split open and we tumbled onto the floor where we rolled around, with me grabbing for Zac's arm. Then someone else got hold of Zac from the other side. Richard. Zac clunked against the remains of the coach, knocking his head.

Zac was suddenly lying still, looking dazed, but the glove went on clenching and flexing. Everyone was staring at it.

"Get the glove off him before he gets up!" I panted.

"Shona, I really think –" began Mr Costello.

"Just do it!" I shouted. Mr Costello's face did a kind of horrified twitch. "Please, please," I begged. "Just help me get it off him."

They must have heard the desperation in my voice. Molly and Richard pulled two fingers each. I grabbed the thumb. Ella held Zac's legs. I must have looked just as mad as Zac.

With a **thwupppp**, the glove came free.

Zac began moaning.

I snatched the glove and jumped off the stage.

I rammed it in my rucksack.

"Sorry everyone. I … I …
gotta go!" I shouted and
dashed out of
the hall.

Chapter 4

I ran home, my head spinning with all
that Zac had said and done in the play
rehearsal.

"My gauntlet lives on," he'd said,

"waiting to re-ignite the past." Was the glove turning Zac into a real highwayman?

I flung open the front door and ran through to the kitchen. Mum and Dillon were at the table.

"Shona!" Mum called. "Are you all right?"

"Won't be long!" I called, heading for the garden.

I would bury the glove. That way, Zac couldn't have it. Or smell it. Not if it was under the ground. I grabbed a spade from the shed. Dad had been gardening, so I found a soft bit of soil he'd already cleared and started digging.

"Wotcha doing?" came a chirpy voice. Dillon. I could see him out of the corner of my eye, frisking round me.

But I went on shovelling. Three, four, five huge spadesful landed on the ground at the side. Must make it deep enough.

"Dillon, go away. I'm busy."

When I was satisfied with the hole, I straightened up and stretched.

I glanced back at our garden gate. A cloaked figure was standing behind it. I gasped and dropped the spade. There he stood in his mask, his flashing eyes fixed on me. Zac. But not like Zac; like a terrible dark stranger.

I tore my eyes away, and spun round looking for my rucksack with the glove in. Where was it? I'd put it on the grass next to me! I looked back at the gate. The figure was gone.

Had he ever been there?

Was I going mad?

I rushed inside the house. Mum was on her own at the table now.

"Where's Dillon?" I said.

"I told him to get his shoes from his bedroom."

I belted upstairs. There was no one there.

I heard the front door slam.

I ran down the stairs.

"Well, that was nice, Shona."

I stared at Mum, my heart hammering. "What's nice?"

Mum smiled and held out a plate of biscuits. "It was sweet really. Zac dropped by. Haven't seen him for ages. He was still in his costume, actually. Rather splendid. He's taken Dillon off to the park."

I gaped at her.

"My rucksack, Mum. Did Dillon take it with him?"

"I didn't really notice, love. Sorry. Oh, maybe he *was* carrying something."

I stared at her wide smile, my hopes sinking. Zac had got the glove back. And he'd taken Dillon, too.

Chapter 5

About half an hour had passed since Zac had taken Dillon. I kept puzzling over it in my head; Zac certainly didn't care about me, so what would he want with Dillon?

At least I knew where to find them. And I'd got an idea how to trick Zac. After all, he was hardly going to just whip off the glove and hand it over, was he?

My first job was to collect a packet of white powder that was among the special things I'd put in the coffin-box after Zac had taken the glove out of it.

Then I set off to the common, going a long way round so that I passed the site of The Noose and Gibbet pub where we'd found the glove weeks ago. I had to check something.

The trees loomed over my head as I set off across the common in the evening light. I clambered over a fallen tree near the stream and remembered all the times Zak and I had made dams with branches. We'd spent such a lot of time together over the years, but now the glove was making him into a stranger. I had to put it out of his reach for ever.

I picked my way through the tangle of brambles, skewering myself on a holly bush as I swung off the path towards the middle of the common. My footsteps were soundless on the soft grass.

I saw some smoke swirling up – we'd made bonfires and built shelters on the common when were in the Scouts.

That's when Zac and I had
first found the tree struck by
lightning. It had been split
open, leaving a sooty black
hollow where the first big
branches were. The space in
front of it was clear ground; in
summer we left our bikes there.

I slowed down.

A figure sat there now,
staring into a fire. I
stepped nearer, still
camouflaged by the
trees. It was Zac, in
his cape.

As I got closer, I could hear Dillon's voice calling from the back of the tree. "Zac, I don't like it in here. Why don't you talk to me? Please, Zac!"

I skirted round and pushed through the nettles behind the tree, then climbed up to the hollow.

"Dillon," I whispered. I put my finger to my lips. "Shush."

Dillon saw me and grabbed my hand. "Zac said he'd smash my train set if I came out of the tree, Shona," he whispered in a big breath.

"It's all right, Dillon," I whispered. "We're playing a special game; when I say run, we're both going to run. Just wait for the signal. You'll love it."

Dillon's bottom lip was wobbling. "Why is Zac being horrid?" he said.

"Don't worry, Dillon," I said, squeezing his hand. "I'll sort it. I'll be back in a minute."

I walked back round to the front of the tree.

"Zac," I said.

Zac sprang up. "Well, well!" Firelight danced across his eyes.

"I've come to join you, Zac."

"You jest!" Zac said, striding up to me, but I could tell he was curious.

I felt his gloved hand settle on my shoulder. My gaze flicked to the tree. I could just make out Dillon's little face gleaming out at me in the dusk. Zac squeezed my shoulder and I felt the glove move up to my neck.

"Why would you want to join me?" Zac said softly, raising an eyebrow.

"You're special, Zac," I squeaked, my heart hammering as I felt the leathery fingers resting against my neck. "You are …" I coughed, terror rising in my chest. "You're a legend!"

Zac's hand fell away. "A legend," he murmured.

I breathed out a massive breath.

"Sit!" he said.

We sat.

Zac poked at something that was roasting over the fire.

"Life on the run will be lonely with only the owls calling in the dead of night," Zac muttered. He looked at me without blinking.

There were dark shadows under his eyes. His skin was pale and dusty. And the deep frown. The real Zac never frowned. His face was always somewhere between one laugh and the next.

The fire crackled. My stomach lurched. I kept finding my eyes wandering back to whatever was roasting over the fire.

"I need a horse," Zac said.

I looked down at my shaking hands.

"A horse! Yes, great idea," I heard myself say.

I eased the white packet out of my pocket. Zac's gloved arm was next to me, his fingers resting on the ground, clenching and unclenching.

He sighed. "You are not afraid, are you?"

His unblinking eyes rested on me again.

No, petrified, I wanted to shout.

Zac looked up at the dark trees. "If you betray me, you will suffer," he said gruffly.

I looked down. There, right next to me, was his arm, inside the highwayman's glove. The wide cuff gaped. Wide enough! I held the packet clenched between my finger and thumb.

Super Strong Itching Powder. It's made of tiny burrs. Hooks.

I tore off the top, hiding the noise with a short cough. I prayed Zac wouldn't look at my shaking hands. I swiftly emptied the entire packet down the glove. The fingers flexed restlessly but Zac didn't look down. I breathed out slowly.

We gazed up at the sky, the highwayman and I.

I prayed for the powder to work.

Zac's mouth twitched. A flicker crossed his face.

Suddenly, he looked at the glove and roared, "Argh! What is happening?" He began hitting his arm with the fist of his other hand.

"Something is biting me!" Zac snatched up a stick from the ground and thrust one end inside his glove.

"I will not take it off. I will not take it off! I will not! I will not!" he moaned. "The pain, the pain!" he panted, his whole face contorted in agony.

Just then Dillon shouted. "Is it now when we run, Shona?"

Zac wheeled round and rushed to the back of the tree. Dillon was perched up in the hollow, looking eager for the game to begin.

Panic thrilled through me. It had all gone wrong. Zac jumped up at the tree, trying to grab Dillon, reaching up with his gloved arm into the hollow.

"Argh!" Dillon screamed. "What's the matter with Zac? He's doing a horrid face at me!"

"You pathetic small … argh!" Zac's voice changed to a high yelp. His arm had got stuck in a cleft in the hollow. I jumped up at his body, trying to pull him away.

For a second, Zac hung there by the glove, then came the **thwuck** as his hand pulled free and he fell to the ground. The glove tumbled after him.

Zac began tearing at the skin of his bare hand. "The itching, the itching … Argh! Water!" he yelled, rushing away down the slope towards the stream.

"Now, Dillon!" I shouted, snatching up the glove.

As Dillon scrambled down the tree, I grabbed his hand and we dashed away through the undergrowth.

"Too fast, Shona!" Dillon panted.

"Come on," I panted back. "You can do it."

In a few seconds we were out of the common and on the road.

As we ran past the parade of shops, I glanced back. Zac was running after us, the highwayman's cape streaming out behind him. He shook his fist at me.

"Give it back!" he yelled.

"This is fun!" squealed Dillon as we dodged some wheelie bins on the pavement. Then I had a brilliant idea – wheelie bins! I turned, grabbed one and spun it across the pavement behind me. We ran on but there was soon a massive crash as Zac was sent flying.

"Come on, Dillon!" I shouted, yanking his arm. "Not far now!"

We ran across the roundabout and along the road. I had to be far enough ahead for my plan to work!

Chapter 6

There was nothing left of the old pub
now but rubble and a few yellow-jacketed
builders working on in the fading light.
Nothing left of the bar inside, where we'd
found the evil glove. The whole place had
been completely flattened. A digger had
opened up a huge pit for the foundations
of a new building.

Dillon and I ran through the gateway
and jumped over the cones.

Grey goo was flowing down the chute from a giant cylinder as three builders shouted up instructions and raked over the top. They hadn't noticed me yet and, by the time they did, it would all be over.

I held up the highwayman's glove.

"Go back to where you came from!" I shouted.

I hurled the black glove with every ounce of energy I had left. It went spinning though the air, and then dropped down into the goo as the next grey waterfall tumbled down from the mixer. The porridgy mix surged round the glove, rolling it over and over.

Zac appeared, panting beside me.

"You're too late!" I called, pointing to the concrete.

The surface rippled and we gasped as something burst through, forcing a tidal wave on both sides. The sky went dark as if a storm were about to break, and the air turned cold. A murky shape rose up from deep in the trench.

"What's that?" Dillon called. "Ugh! Look!"

It was an arm.

I grabbed hold of Dillon and Zac on either side of me. We clung together, mesmerized by what we saw.

The arm moved towards the glove and its fingers closed around it. Then it raised the glove aloft and seemed to turn towards us. It gave one defiant shake, and then sank back under the grey concrete mixture that surged back. All that remained was a little hiccup on the surface of the sludge. Then that flattened out into stillness.

The sky cleared and everything seemed to lighten. The three of us stood gazing down the slope into the still concrete.

Time seemed to stop.

In the end, it was Zac who spoke.

"Are you OK, Shona?" he asked quietly.

"Yeah," I said. "You?"

Zac paused then nodded slowly.

"This was where the highwayman was hanged," I murmured. "That's why they called the pub The Noose and Gibbet." I shuddered. "This is where the gallows was."

"What was that thing," Dillon whispered, "in the grey stuff?"

"I don't know," I said. "It's gone, Dillon. Whatever it was, it's gone."

Dillon looked at me, wide-eyed. "Was it watching us?"

"I'm not sure," I said slowly. "Long ago, a bad person died here, Dillon. He hurt people. He made them miserable. He wore the glove, and that glove still seemed to have some of his evil power, even today."

Zac called, "Come on, Dillon. He's welcome to that old glove, isn't he?"

I looked round at Zac. He was smiling – he looked like his old self. He leap-frogged over a pile of bricks and then grabbed me to come and do it too.

"I'm starving," he said. "Who fancies some chips?"

Dillon looked back anxiously at the concrete. I took his hand.

"It's all right, Dillon. The game's over," I said.

And we ran chasing and laughing back down the road towards home.